In Deep Time – Connemara

Ita O'Donovan

Ita O'Donovan

First Published in 2017
Reprint 2019

The Knocknarone Press
Maum
Clifden
County Galway
Ireland
knocknaronepress@gmail.com

Layout and cover design: Tom Hunter

Printed by Clódóirí CL Print, Casla and Moycullen,
www.clprint.ie

ISBN 978-1-5272-1592-4

Ita O'Donovan

Ita O'Donovan was born in Cork City and now lives in Errislannan near Clifden, County Galway. Her work has been published in a number of magazines, anthologies, newspapers and in a biography. She has won the Mid West North West Poetry Prize, was highly commended in Strokestown International Poetry Prize and shortlisted in the Allingham Poetry Competition and in *The Irish Times*, Hennessy New Irish Writing

Acknowledgements

Acknowledgements are due to the editors of *Poetry Ireland Review, The SHop, Southword, Skylight Poetry, Jumping the Bus Queue* and *Clifden Writers' Group Anthology*, where versions of some of these poems were first published; and to Connemara Community Radio where some were broadcast.

I wish to thank the members of Clifden Writers' Group for their constructive comments, encouragement and friendship for over 20 years. Sincere gratitude is extended to my poetry workshop colleagues, Robyn Rowland, Eileen Keane and Art Ó'Súilleabháin for the mutual criticism and discussion of our work. I offer special thanks to Tony Curtis for reading the manuscript and for his insightful response to it. I want to express my deep and warmest appreciation to Robyn Rowland for her belief in this book, her editing and generous sharing of her time and expertise in crafting it into a format ready for publishing. She is truly inspirational.

Contents

for John

Derrigimlagh Bog

The road is hedged with bursts of gold
drifting a faint smell of coconut,
senses are heightened
before I enter a landscape of subtlety and nuance.

I reach the bog stretching out low into unhindered wind,
except where stark rock emerges – outcrops
of a high grey table or gables like a stone house,
sheltering a canny sheep, legs tucked under.

Watching the others flow over rough terrain,
sturdy white fleeces on delicate black legs,
I hear the ripping velcro sound
as black matching heads busily crop, crop.

The washed out beiges and ochres of winter
are slowly greening, soon brushed with muted colours
of sphagnum moss, heather, sedges,
fragile cotton and purple moor grass.

Low hummocks and hollows are broken
by patterned pools. I pass one
edged with silver flashes,
the surface moved as if by a biblical wind.

Skylarks are rising,
vibrating crescendos of feathers,
piercing the air
with their song of unlimited joy.

I am walking in deep time, layered over four thousand years.
If you sink a corer, each section yields five centuries.
You can read the stories, the history and the pollen,
a preserved manuscript.

The Archaeologists

They'll wonder why I kept five stones,
each a little bigger than a walnut,
notched and with eroded facets,
comfortable to hold, but not too smooth
as would make them hard to catch,
like the nuances in the everyday phrases
that we've said most to one another.
They've never seen the marble doorstep,
which feet had worn to a shallow saucer.
There I scattered the stones
before I flung one up to begin
the complex game of fives or gobs,
its rules and rhymes
passed on and on by rote.
Sweep the kitchen, pick up the chair,
sweep underneath it and put it down there.
There was always one gob in the air
that you were never sure of catching.

Filature

Filature – the reeling of silks from cocoons,
barely invisible threads
dew-beaded with tears
dropping down like a spider's escape.

Spun and coloured rubia, amber, indigo,
a rainbow's reflection
vibrating as when the wind
chimes an Aeolian harp.

Crafted into a coat of journeys,
a hat of significance,
a quilt of remembrance,
a child's comforter.

Totem Pole

Silvered, distressed, this piece of driftwood's
in a shape that's curved with a rotund bum.
Cleft here and there and here with a deep cut
as if by an adze, some outlines are scratched in –
this could be a stoat flowing into a drystone wall
or this a swift in flight, free, ecstatic,
these marks as if patient laboured lines
in the first alphabetic script of Bacchylides' poems.
In parts there's a smoothness where the tides
have rocked it gently to and fro, to and fro,
before carrying it high
where sands blow grounds of time
to erode and cover over
this bleached cadaver
on Curhownagh strand.

December in Errislannan

Chaste it was and clear. Morning quiet,
so still it seemed dawn was afraid to kiss
the sea and wake it. Neptune would riot
and cry, crash high to create an abyss,
and ships would slide and whoosh down seaweed trees
and waving coral fronds. All is in tune
with the splash, gurgle and lap that appease
a crazy, cross God Sea-Man. Shhh, it's noon
and on the tide, dark and sparkling crystal,
float two swans. White Mountains stark in the far
edge of the day. Ice breaks with a pistol
ricochet and bounces back from a star.
I plug the kettle in and muse on a year
gone like snow. Only today is ambered here.

The Mason's Stroke

Seamus Murphy, Sculptor, 1910-1977

Impregnated with dust
and a feeling for stone
relayed through the quarries
by men like The Gargoyle,
Jackdaw or Blueskull.
There is no regularity in nature,
they said,
as the tulip wilted
while you struggled to carve it
on a soft block,
until they showed the new apprentice
how to keep pressure on the little finger.
In serried order you laid out
fire-sharp chisels, hammers and a rubstone
for your first job – a marble pulpit for Fermoy.
Danny Melt put a section of it on your banker
and swept away the spalls.
You talked headstones over beer
and how the Granite Fusilier
carved the Honan Chapel.
Your sculptor's reputation
grew Monumental Boy
despite yourself.
Before you went to London and Paris,
you learned the secret language of stone
and broke open its silence.

Courtship

Time we spend together is agate time –
bands of colour, exquisite balance.
You trace stars on my cheek to divert me,
your deep brown voice and eyes captivate
so I trail a decoy bird-wing and flirt a little.
Desire becomes a maelstrom of aching want,
yet contentment is layered as schist is in rock.
I dry crystals from your skin after laughing in the sea.
Spare, like something precious,
I break a fragment of love and place it on your tongue.
I tease the texture of your hollows,
an advent preparation for the feast.
Celestes, please play iridescent music to the moon,
celebrate, before the tide ebbs too soon.

Birth Days

On the radio,
the distinctive northern voice
cantillates his poems in birthday celebration.
I hunker in my space absorbing,
the burr, the cadence.

A knock on the glass door.
Did Heaney write anything about lettuce?
You, my love,
in your battered boots, holed jumper
and slowing steps.

I find the packets for you, lolla rossa,
buttercrunch and burnet.
Leaving the poet, I record their names
as you take seeds between thumb and finger
and drop them in the opened earth.

You move to cover them in their dark blanket,
knees reluctant on a square of plywood,
then firm-in re-cycled strips of wood
to mark the harvest, naming them
with a pen impervious to rain and salt.

I mind an urgent baptism
when we were lithe and quick
but anguished,
me blood-staunched, you rock steady,
as we sped the long road to hospital.

Our first seed germinated still in my womb,
we chose, discarded, settled
on a boy's name, a girl's name.
A son was born,
his breath precarious,

but he held fast,
the psalmist's first olive shoot
around the kitchen table,
its surface now like a story,
marked and grooved in Ogham.

Aillebrack

We plash like kids
then stand a while,
our ankles assessing
the piercing at the floor
of a pellucid sea lit by sunlight.
Nodules of seaweed in heart shapes
and glossy tawny strings float by.
In the distance a toddler with
her granny in rolled-up jeans
hold hands and, with little rushes,
dare the tide.
Connemara ponies follow nose to tail
along the coastal path,
their riders galloping them on,
on to the machair to crush pink clover
and lady's bedstraw – honey-smelling.
At last we totally immerse,
cry out with that mixture of fear and joy
at returning to our first known element
until the bay becomes our familiar,
and through clear water
we explore our under-world.
Then, pushing against a resistant sea
to the stretched shore,
we find translucent domes – half-bubbles
scattered along the ebb-tide line.
We pick our way,
just looking,
we don't want this to be the day
the fragile shining bursts.

Found in Ballinahinch Wood

Robert Frost was on my mind today.
Unlike his silver birch,
this one is standing
tall and smooth and straight
like a young girl not yet budded,
or a boy's young body, still pliant,
unbowed by western storms.
Nearby, hugging earth,
the remains of a fallen tree
has a carapace of roughened bark,
where adhesions of stray growth
have found a home.

Further in, the pattern on the river replicates
the considered marks of a Le Brocquy tapestry.
There is an ambiguous plop in the water
and far above the wind-zither plays the leaves.
The birds are not insistent
as if overawed by ancient time,
visible in the roots twisting on the path
polished by many feet
and in the stepping stones gathered, bedded-in,
by hands in another century.
A waterfall of moss
with slow velvet fertility
seems thrown there to soften my eyes.
There's a muffled musk of leaf mould
and stilled life of the insect world,
a compost for renewal.

Spaces in Between

after a painting by Alannah Robins

I am the silence
between two heartbeats,
the lapse of time
between one word and another.

I am shape also
within the gleaming silver tracery
strolled by a snail on patio flags
or the blue gap between clouds.

See me in between a flight of starlings,
fluid, swift and ever-changing.
I am instinctive and careful between horses,
even when they thunder in a herd.

You see me in the distance between each human,
if there is betrayal my borders will be walled off.
If, of one heart with all, a gate will be left open,
if loved by another, boundaries will be dismantled.

Impressions

On the horizon, temples of my mind,
a mountain range that is a mandala.
Colours of ivory and almandine
and the soft wind's musk-pear fragrance
brush the sea's surface and quaking sand.
My footprints follow my uncertain dance
until the moon calls time and the tide-wave
scatters grains over them in evening-land.

In morning-land millions of years ago
Lucy left her footprints – not in the snow –
but fossilised in black volcanic ash.
Pollen-tubes spoke of meadows and no trees
for aerial roads – she stood up and walked.
In that leap of imagination Lucy left her imprint.

Anchor Rock

My lover stands
hosing down a blue trailer.
Like Hercules, twelve tasks
are planned and carried through.

He helped Martin lift blocks,
timbers for the roof,
slates for the beams,
and a skylight for the sky.

Then like a child's drawing
he made the garden,
though wielding a garden tool
is tougher than a pen.

Alders for birds,
the old well,
hydrangeas to riot colour,
shrub roses to tumble red petals.

The circle of water
includes the moon,
includes the sun,
silver morning, golden evening.

A Praise Poem

for John

Curled on a cushioned rock
you've carved out for me,
there's an incessant humming,
busy until a bumble bee
full stops with a buzz.
Errisbeg mounts to a blue sky.
Little puppet dolls on your fuchsia
dance in scarlet, as another bee
dives into the bell of an orange nasturtium.
There's a whirr of blurred wings
and a commentary from the occasional finch
before he flies in arabesques.
Sun in September creates urgency
yet the sea is lazy,
hardly brimming under seaweed.

It's everything you want to seal in a globe
to shake in the grey winter,
after we've gathered your honey,
bee and I.

On this Day

The road catnaps,
tide steals in.
John has cut the grass.
The growl of the mower
is a grub's up call
to Blackbirds.
I look out and watch one,
concentration in every feather
as he cocks an ear to hear
and with a hop
arrows his beak
before the worm has time to turn.
Out of blue air a drove of leverets
bound into the field.
I count five.
One hunkers down to nibble,
others play statues,
antennae ears erect
like exclamation marks.
They race in a game of tag
kicking their heels in high jinks,
like children playing.

I ponder on news this morning
from a keening land.
A story of Arab boys,
young Pelés, eyes on the ball,
bodies tense with effort,
crying *shoot, shoot,*
near make-shift goalposts.
Small bodies, bare legs,
they run between scattered debris.

There's a sweet-sour smell
of rotting garbage, a mecca
for prowling cats.
Brothers and cousins,
who, confined like rabbits in a burrow
to keep them safe,
today slipped out. They collected each other
to straggle to their playspace by the shore,
their kinship stronger
than the bonding of a world cup team.
But across the bay the air crackles,
death-whistles pierce the sky,
artillery salvos
blowing one, then three, to smithereens.

Out on the sea
Gunner A
refocuses his gun.
Shrugs.

Basilica de Saint Nazaire, Carcassonne

Prayer heaped on prayer,
building a steeple reaching to the sky.
Two rose-windows, stained glass
deepest blues and purple at the North
intense carmine and yellow at the South,
here you must follow the path of the sun
to be lanced by light.

The pilgrims from Croatia
crowd the church,
their fervour reverberates
against grey gothic arches.
The organist rolls massive waves of sound,
a crescendo to heaven.
I find a small space
to light a candle for a friend,
always a flickering sign of hope,
even where the stones are saturated
with cries of despair,
centuries of appeal.

A Baroque Night in Clifden

– In Christ Church

Rough stones forever fingerprinted
in the practised eyeing of the space,
selection, dressing and heisting in place
by, who knows, perhaps Festy, Martin or Henry,
the stone men building there in eighteen fifty-three.

To the rise and fall of intended compliments,
the *Akademie* lift their instruments.
Holding a child-sized fiddle
crafted in the time of Handel,
Bernhard's tall frame dances
as his lighter bow glances
off the strings – the thinner sound
recalling the fiddler in the story
lured to play in the rath, a faery ground.
Christine long bows the melody
on a graver violin.

Raphael on harpsichord,
Barbara on cello,
Bjorn on theorbo,
weave basso continuo
with ornamented rococo,
now dolce now staccato,
the plucked notes of the baroque guitar
dark chocolate bass.
Musicians eyeing space,
selecting, dressing notes,
fingering them into place,
mirror the calloused hands of Festy, Martin and Henry,
who ensured that stones return sound fairly,
granite's perfect pitch echoing.

and I pronounce you separate man and separate woman – the woman's response

and the nights when the moon and stars were up there colliding;
and our four warm bundles, snuggle-eyed, grónáning,
each in turn a mighty wonder;
and my exhausted head on your lap and you caressing it;
and the day all the wellingtons were left on the island strand
like tree stumps from a sunken forest,
and you bending, oars lifting and dripping,
as we rowed back in silence;
and the day you went fishing with your brothers,
they having helped you first to paint the house,
and the singing over the water as the engine putted home,
but with no salmon in the boat;
and the screeching rush to Casualty,
me holding Mickey's limp body, his eyelids fluttering at last
and our hopes rising as we reached the gate;
and your mother and sister holding the fort
when we flew to Paris,
a blue-hazed city that called out to all our joyful senses;
and me polishing your grandmother's brass candlesticks
for your father's wake;
and my sister's party when a tumbling brood of youngsters,
twelve cousins, as alike and unalike
as pebbles on a beach,
sang and danced for us;
my bright dear heart, death would have been the easy parting.
Now there is the slow painful picking apart
of the strands of our life,
the warp and now the weft.
Before I take hold of the dreaded spear of Scawtha
with its thirty sharp-wounding spikes or raise a curse on you,
my love, come let us take the needle and unpick that last thread.

Drowning

I was much further out than you thought
– Stevie Smith

I hadn't slept Monday.
I hadn't slept Tuesday.
Wednesday night I read
Gone with the Wind
volume one.
On Thursday night I tossed and turned
all three hundred and twenty pages
of volume two.
On Friday, you said,
I never want to see that bloody book again.
I didn't wake up next morning,
I just got up
to the gloom of another day,
each action
a mountain of shale
to be climbed slowly
with no touchstone to guide me.
There was thick silence in my head,
I watched lips on faces
move to their mouth-corners,
to show smiling teeth.
I wondered how they did it.
I had forgotten how to laugh.
I kept slipping back,
dislodging fragments of myself
which bounced from rock to rock
echoing all the way down.
When light filtered through
there was no horizon.

Daybreak

When I finger my worry beads,
over life playing hardball
with my children, say,
the texture gets smoothed
quicker than my thoughts.
Darkness seeps in like mist,
finding all the vulnerable depressions.
The day becomes inscrutable,
nothing is written on it yet.
Clouds mock me
using chiaroscuro, switching between
light and no light
before drawing black-out curtains
to heighten fears.
When there's a break in their scudding forms,
I see the man-in-the-moon
sleeping tonight in his hammock
relaxed and holding most of his light
for elsewhere.
Comes morning, dawn takes charge,
a security cordon pushing back
the crowd of dark in my thoughts.
Rain has varnished the stones
which now gleam in the light
creeping serenely into the day
and into the crevices of my mind.

Soul Spirits

i.m. Barbara Callan

That time is measured
is of no consequence
in the praise flutterings
of a butterfly
as it adorns a day.
Flashes of cerulean blue
or orange-frilled white,
fritillaries effervescing in sun-drenched air,
an exultate to be imagined
not touched,
as a frisson of legs hooks onto your finger,
wings close in a silent clap.

Echoing Silence

after The Ryan Report into Child Abuse 2009

This is a museum
where archaeologists are still working,
piecing together what went before,
holding a fragment in their hands
feeling the cold of it,
letting their mind into the life
so they can complete the image,
the fresco of one moment.
A boy is in it, he is in distress.
They do not find his tears.

Years are spent searching,
papers rustling, notes made,
comparing this with that,
trying to extract meaning
from the hieroglyphs of a system,
but they cannot capture
the sounds the boy hears,
sounds he cannot forget.

They get weary in this museum,
puzzled with the God of that time
who had different faces,
presenting sun only to some
and darkness always to others.
There were cult disciples of the darkness,
who penned in children for sacrifice.
The disciples of the sun cult
looked the other way.
The girls in the damaged fresco
hold hands out as if in supplication.

In the museum, they work on,
lights beaming out late at night.
They call in artists
to honour their work,
The Book of Harrowed Hours.
A Book to record
what could never all be found
what could never all be heard
what could never all be sensed
what could never all be forgiven.

A Seaweed Cornucopia

Hair of mermaid and her purse,
I gild the sea, ebb like yesterday with the tide.
I am rose madder fronds, lime green threads
thrown up on sand like a child's discarded toys.
I slitherslip a camouflage on rocks,
tide-mark the margins of bays and tang the air with ancient myrrh.
With *meireanach* and *coirleach*, I enrich the land
and provide sustenance with carrageen, dulse and laver.
Whom the tide takes I sigh over with shelled skeins
of horned wrack, bladderwrack and kelp.

Underwater I am translucent in sunlight on still seas.
I weave fringed kilims to decorate surface of oceans
and ornament with my red rags, furbelows or peacock's tail.
I make rococo mirrors with molten sea for cumulus and Orion.
I seduce with thongweed or dabberlocks,
in a sea queen's bath I lave skin soft.
I enamel the ocean with olive, garnet, ruby and topaz.
I sculpt a storm on the strand
with heavy batons torn in anger by a frenzied Neptune
and left piled high by a retreating, exhausted sea.
An equinox harvest,
a gift of the moon.

Fand

Mannanán Mac Lir's lament for his unfaithful queen

She was the storm that rattled my bones.
Oh the pain.
Yet her body was ripeness
which I split like an apple for seeds.
For me she was music,
music that thundered down cliffs.
For me she was the reason the sky silvered,
the world closed
and there was only her and me.
She didn't know that I was the reason
rats ran for cover.
I was the reason children shrivelled
and when I walked in there was a silence
louder than no sound.
Yet after she left
they told me she said
I hear him still
I hear him still.

The Decades of Summer

Summer is
the ooze of cool wet mud
between bare feet.
It's the click click
of childhood grasshoppers,
the prick of thorn on thumb
as a blackberry is unplugged,
the toffee edges
of a berry-apple tart.
It's the promise of it all
being the same next year.

It's the day
that seems forever
when the wind brushed the skin
of two young lovers,
riffling the grass
in the sunlit hollow
where we shared wine and kisses.

It's the busy seasons with our children,
drying off sand between toes,
tying runners,
tying slip-knots of love,
time no longer endless
now it's shared in widening circles,
a promise thrown in a pool.

Summer is the first test-flight from the nest,
the call collect
and money order to strange places;
the joy of summer weddings,
floaty frocks and pretty hats.
It's making a first sandcastle
for a grandchild,
then pressing her velcro sandals
with the loops and burrs that bind.
It's watching the promise
of her flowering.

Summer hurries and scurries
but now our book of hours is slow.
There's time to listen
to the song of hedgerows,
green and cream
scattered with notes of buttercup gold,
chorales of daisy white,
the constant hum of bees gathering nectar,
moments to inhale the musk of old roses
and feel the impregnated heat of a rock.
Yet between stillness in today's dawn
and the glory blaze of sunset,
there's still a promise.

The Cathach of Ronan

for my grandchildren

A square envelope in the post.
I open a card enamelled
with plum-red, copper-green,
yellow tempera
and a patina of smudges.
I can see Ronan at six – plump fingers
grasping the crayon, ignoring the cat,
tracing each letter as he calls,
What comes after B?
A perfection of love
like the synthesis of saltire and diamond
to form a two strand helix,
the serifs, spirals, knotwork,
and the lion swallowing its tail
red dotted by the monk in the scriptorium.

Love comes in Edgeways

for John

My husband in the garden
digs and double digs the earth,
the turning of sods
a procession of small angles.
His foot presses the straight-sided blade,
there is a clink of stone.
Now as the field slopes to the sea,
green is broken by a dark rectangle
where rhubarb will probe winter's dreams.
When the soil warms, it will cradle seeds
as I have cradled his.

The rhubarb reddens and grows ripe,
we taste it in sweet-sour communion.
We harvest strawberries to offer each other
as once I popped grapes in his mouth
on Rosbeigh strand five decades ago.
We sip wine from a calyx
easing aches of body, pain of mind,
toasting our journey in the Noosphere,
the layer of life
that powers reflective thought.
Time melds.

There and Not There

The day's opening is breathless, aware.
Spiders have been busy
spinning a tensile thread
to throw across corners,
creating webs against time.
I'm at the window with coffee,
mind idling, waiting for thought,
when I see the lion.
An accomplished leap
and his haunches squat on the lower wall,
his shoulders and head at ease
but erect on the stone pillar.
His mane is so dark it looks black,
though the rising light
picks out gold on his body.

I've always wanted a lion on our pillar,
not a triumphant eagle,
not a stylite monk to make me feel guilty,
not even a welcoming pineapple.
Beware you might get your wish, Nanny said,
except I never had a Nanny,
not even a St. Bernard called Nana.

The creature is so intense, as if in contemplation,
repeating a mantra,
magnificent, magnificent, magnificent.
Through the open window,
I hear voices, a flow of one, then the other,
then the two together.
A pair of women walkers pass by,
light-stepping to hide stress
as they reach mile six of the circle of Errislannan.
They look towards each other,
seeming not to register the lion,
even though his tail is twitching,
his shoulders crouching as if to pounce.

I renew my coffee.
The smell is piquant but strange.
I look at the packet, Fairtrade Ethiopian.
It's their *hidden treasure.*
I google Lions Ethiopian –
barely-black manes make these
unique to a country
whose favourite proverb is –
if spider webs unite they can tie up a lion.

Third Age Friendship

for Pat O'Connell 1924-2016

Do you mind that I borrowed your heron?
He poses like stone before loud flapping
take-off wings announces his desertion
of my inlet. Now the tide is brimming,
you and I will swim in the glass depths below your house,
where no ribbons of seaweed will tangle
mer-legs like a slimy octopus.
Is it the salt, or the red sun's angle
on the sea, or strains of Thelonius
Monk that make our after-swim drinks zing?
We'll talk of Monet, Apollonius,
and why Patsy D'Arcy's van is passing
at after two o'clock instead of one.

Flight Bag to Villa Zacconi

Next week I'll fly to the landscape
of Da Vinci and Raphael,
brown but with evergreen cypress
still etching conical towers.
But now outside, sun is glinting
on the pebbled mud-ebb.
It gleams on squares of chicken wire,
in beads of rain on grass
and on the spread of rhubarb leaves,
the conversation of the day
between sunshine and shower cloud.

The scattered trees are bent
to commands of western gales.
There are ghost whispers
from the two rocks I watch
that measure the tide,
and an eyeless ruin, stone gables
stoically erect,
that measures loss.
These are the stories of my landscape.
Like the legend of Mannanán,
I'll take their language in my travel purse.

Villa Zacconi

for Sara

The landscape surprises with its shades of lush green.
Trees guard the villa,
last bastion before the Apuan Alps,
mountains that today march towards us.
They catch passing clouds to pierce a deluge.
Sometimes, the wind blows soft coils of white
and a sudden arc of sunlight picks out a village
clinging by its fingertips,
before lighting up another.
Bells chime from the valley, air-muffled.
Birds fly and sing, sing and fly.
There is a high note of jasmine.

In this Art Deco house of an actor
there is a slow dance,
six women in search of the breaking of bread
and later the drinking of wine,
six unfinished characters in search of a choral ode.
Laughter spools from threads of many colours.
Stories woven are part of the gospel according to woman,
wise, wounded, weary, whimsical, wonderful.
No more than for Pirandello, they don't need a poet.

Within Salzburg Salt Mine

There is only one way down.
All arrayed in white
our group is gathered
inside the mountain top.
We straddle behind one another
on the miners' wooden slide,
legs outside legs
like a strange centipede.
The brake is released,
no way back.
Fear isolates.
This is a journey I face alone.
We shoot down a white surface,
the friction burn I feel
when I trail my hand
like the memory of my son
hurtling down the birth canal.
The slide comes to a halt
beside a lake suffused with greenish light
reflecting off stalactites
and stalagmites in phallic shapes.
A beam is lifted
to release the small wooden door.
We are ushered into bright summer light
on a meadow woven with wild-flowers,
blue gentians, purple vetch, yellow of cowslips
and bellflowers, a shock of colour after white.
I look up at the mountain
enclosing a salt mine,
where slaves once laboured.

It leaves a shiver.

The wheels on the bus go round and round

The bus moved in off the road.
Thanks, Simon, the countrywoman said,
chatting as she went down the step,
it won't be the coffee pot
but the Wellingtons and the spade,
that's for sure, when I reach the door.

We watched her stride for her blue door,
our lights still visible from the road,
wondering what she dug with that spade.
Please to stop at the cross, the man said,
with the strange hat shaped like a pot,
a foreign man. He lunged down the step,

going into the dark he missed his step,
far from home, the colour of the door
not the red of childhood, missing the pot
of sunflowers, poppies wild on the road.
There was always coffee, he said,
bubbling on the stove. The spade,

that was there too, my grandpapa's spade.
It was always left near the step
to dig or chase dogs with. So he had said
as that woman went to her door,
before he too went out on the road
with bags and his strange hat like a pot.

Coffee be damned – tea made in a teapot,
good and strong, as black as the spade
I trumped with last night. No road
for them to go, one more step
and I won the game of 45. Out the door
with me then, the thin man said.

You're a terrible man, Simon said,
you should have stayed, you won the pot.
Finders keepers, echoed back through the door,
as the Cardsharp reached home. No spade
for him but a cosy house just a step
from shops. The bus sped down the road.

Mind the step, Simon said.
I opened a door like Alice
and was out on the road with a pot and a spade.

for I will consider the heavens in Mannin Bay

I looked up and there they were,
Jupiter and Saturn, brideboys
lighting the way like postilions
about to be struck by lightning.

Jupiter and Saturn, the brideboys,
and here comes the bride
slipping from behind an arras,
the silver-edged cloud trailing like Ophelia.

And here comes the bride,
millions and trillions of candlepower
driving us mad with light,
turning grey night ethereal.

Millions and trillions of candlepower,
a sphere of beauty
on the run, the run of the heavens,
until Zeus impregnates her in a shower of gold.

Memorial Evening at Errislannan Graveyard

Ovoid stones from Candoolan strand,
smooth-buffeted by Atlantic combers,
are brought here not to raise a cairn
but for ballast on the altar cloth.

Criss-cross greetings fade
among the scattered graves
as Mass commences. The scent
of new cut grass rises like incense.

Time comes to recollect names
from heart whispers.
Michael John calls out Siobháin
taken by the sea, who loved horses.

Later a sudden pounding of hooves
accompanies the priest's chant
as two grey Connemaras
gallop near us to chase a seagull.

As the white bird soars,
it draws our eyes upwards.

Morning

Sit where nature is reclaiming
a stony patch of ground,
a patient invader
sending a vanguard of tall daisies,
with glaring yellow eyes
fringed in white,
jabbing their fingers in triumph.

A butterfly is eddying upon thyme
on his one brief velvet day.
A cuckoo calls and calls its name
as Knocknarone rises on tip-toe
to peer over Mannin Bay.
Peace is shattered by a dumper
throatily reversing to crank up and release
an avalanche of drums and rattles.

I'm reading Philip Larkin's *Aubade*,
life ending in a blank nothing.
But suppose our breath is taken – spellbound?
I open post and read of the death of May.
We shared a whitewashed room
in an Inn at Salzburg,
living like groupies in the shade of Mozart.

Cellos and choirs wove his chords
in and out of gold and cream rococo,
while impish cherubs mocked us from above.
The seeming innocence of a clarinet
moved slowly through descending sequences
before the melody
held us in thrall
to something ephemeral.

One night we gripped our seats,
tense, wondering if the understudy
Queen of the Night
would hit that out-of-world high C.
The hall, so *avant-garde*
inside its ancient carapace,
still holds her lost note.

Our Offshore Islands

I. Inis Airc – The Island of the Shark

An island you can walk around
a few times in one day
is a community
bound to each other
as well as to the sea.
When it's abandoned,
the cries of the birds,
the crash of the siege-guns of the ocean,
the scrape of receding stones
as the tide withdraws,
must echo grief.

The remaining twenty-four islanders,
bereft of the haven of a harbour,
survivors of gales and neglect,
gathered to leave Inis Airc.
On Thursday 20th October 1960,
they left for emigration to the mainland
or flight abroad.
It must have been like the chaos
of a wartime forced march.
Amid the woe,
were hens in baskets,
geese in sacks
and red geraniums sheltered
like the one baby,
eleven months-old, wrapped tight.
There was an iron bedstead,
an iron bath,
cows, sheep, cats, dogs,
ten donkeys and a stack of hay.

It was said
that one of the twenty-four
stayed one more night,
walking the island many times
listening out for his two sons,
lost in the channel
between two islands,
his own and Inishbofin.
Before Thomas left,
he set the table for three,
pulled up three chairs,
and closed the door,
leaving it on the latch.

II. Inis Toirc – The Island of the Wild Boar

i.m. Petey Burke

A place of sheer cliffs and wild ocean,
where if your neighbour's cow was in calf
you supplied his family with milk.
When a cow went 'bogging'
and needed to be hauled out,
you went 'cooring', giving a hand.
You salted ling, foraged for carrageen and cockles
and fished when storms abated.
In the stern of a currach, you held an oar
at right angles in the thole pin,
as you fought to keep the prow to the waves,
save the boat and your three oarsmen.
At night, young and old gathered,
accordions danced and feet jigged.
People always came in the way they went out
through the sheltered,
never the wind door.

When Petey left Inis Toirc for the mainland
to live in a cottage within sound
of the tides in Mannin Bay,
he must have been listening for their voices,
the voices of his island neighbours
on the wind.
There in his turn, he hosted the Stations,
welcoming us with the priest to his kitchen,
the room *furnished and ready*, as the Gospels said of
where bread was first blessed.
Later, chatting over the tea,
I saw a fine photo of Petey
as a young man in naval uniform.
He told us he was recruited
by the Irish Navy's first Commander,
James Morris from nearby Ballinaboy,
who prized the seamanship of islandmen.

Balanced on the picture rail
all around the room,
were St Bridget's Crosses.
Each eve of her feast day,
Petey had crafted the intricate
four-armed cross
with stems of soft-rush.
He made one for every year
since he left his island –
the lines of his elegy.

Last Testament

He kept the place so tidy
Maureen, the Islandwoman, sighed.
It seemed a bare epitaph
for a man scarce a year dead.

I looked out at his neat fields
still with traces of his *iomairí*
where potatoes once marched in wide drills,
and dry-laid walls crafted with air and stones,
where his gimlet eyes had found the perfect fit.

A Walk on the Low Road

for Henry Conneely

The booming wind writes his name on the sea,
the swell on the bay is wide today
driving south. It is the incoming of May
when we can expect the cuckoo storm,
which that grey bird brings in with him.
Between breaths his treble notes are echoing
off the blue granite hill rising
to Lough Salach on Maum.

Sometimes sound resonates
that causes a primeval fear
from some lost memory.
I wonder is it so for the nesting birds.

Lúghnasa

Lúghnasa O'Dee goes out the back
in her Wellington boots,
her lace peignoir hitched up
from trailing on the wetness of gravel,
whose ochres, reds and blues
have been washed bright again.
She feeds the birds of the air
thinking indeed what other birds would there be?
Later she'll sit on the seat
wrested from rock
by her lover swinging a mallet.
His mother looks down
wondering how the Cork woman
got him back to that,
after she working so hard to free him from it.
Lúghnasa will listen
to the sea talking,
to throaty sibilants of a far-away tractor,
to the bees' frenzy.
She knows she's safe in their angry sound
when she deadheads the roses,
though no one has given her
a veil or an ancient hat.
Lúghnasa will pull some lettuce
to thin out the soft green butterhead,
upstanding oak and serrated red leaves.
One day I'll take them to market,
she thinks, to give to people free.

She knows the stallholders won't like it,
but she'll set up next the woman
who could sell rain to a Connemara man,
who'll come, stare, take her share,
then put up a notice –
Free Lettuce with every Buy –
on the big boots with the steel tips,
on the CDs and the jumpers.
Lúghnasa O'Dee has had a bone scan.
It shows a curved spine – just slightly.
Congenital, the nurse says, *there since birth.*
Lúghnasa knows different. She knows
it's sorrows and absences that have made it so.

Chasing a Poem in Ventenac

A sleuth in a battered straw hat in search of a poem
in one small square of sunlight and shadow,
armed with a glass to magnify what is hard to see
and as elusive to capture as a brown lizard
that flashes along a wall to reach a crack of safety.
Here I must dream the creamy lichen on the stone steps
growing by accretion,
must interweave the ping-pong sound of murmured chat,
the harsher sound of a revving engine,
the slick of tyres,
the fluting song of a nightingale
before he burrs,
and the coos of doves
into the warp and weft of a cat's cradle
to use as a poem-catcher
swinging from my four-poster bed.

My familiars are a fly with silver-grey wings
and raised stripe detail on its scarab body,
a white butterfly that flies its drunken random path
but doesn't pause to tickle-land on my hand,
though he blesses me in passing.
Here is the A to Z –
a green shrub whose blossom lies in brown crumb drifts,
near one sere leaf with odd shaped holes weakening its fabric
as when air touches a shroud in a sarcophagus.

Poets have the Best Ideas

for Richard Murphy

Once in Cleggan a poet showed me
round his house of pink granite,
thumb-printed by local craftsmen.
But it's the way he planned the garden
I remember.
He created four bowers,
woven and leafy over time,
each giving shelter
from one of the four winds of Erin
and their mad helter-skelter up the bay,
wild crescendo over the Twelve Bens.

Now I write this out sheltered from the west,
my seat enclosed by the arms of an alder tree
where, no doubt, Mad Sweeney perches,
as is his wont, to intone his lyrics.
Or I can sit sheltered from the north,
where my Connemara man carved
out space in our blue granite
to fit a curved stone seat.
God love him, he's not finished yet,
for when the wind blows
from the east or from the south,
I cannot sit to hatch a poem
to later watch its fledge and flight.

Petition

Achilles washed the gleaming cup and then drew wine.
Pouring a libation to Zeus he intoned a prayer,
his chant pleading for victory over Trojan cohorts
pressing near trenches dug by the Greeks,
and safe return for his beloved Patroclus.
The moon looked down.

Patroclus driving back the hordes was killed.
Even his horses wept hot tears, lowered their heads,
their long manes trailing dust.
Revengeful Achilles slaughtered without pity
before dying at the walls of Troy.
The moon looked down.

The Gods, jealous, bitchy but immortal, ate, drank and played.
They helped their favourites win in combat,
sending mist or fire or holding them back illegally
when Zeus was looking somewhere else.
But they never interfered with fate when death came
as the moon moved through the sky.

And so Zeus and Mars looked here or there
and wars roared on and on.
Now God, or Gods, have different names,
though wars roar on and on,
and they too never interfere with fate.
Each night the moon looks down.

At Gallipoli, near Troy,
behind the lines of battle,
Shaw-Stewart wrote,
Stand in the trench, Achilles,
Flame-capped, and shout for me.
He was felled as the moon rose up.

In Gaza, a man covered in the dust of rubble
begged warrior invaders to rescue his mother,
or let him try. Her legs trapped, she cried for help.
They hardened their hearts and shelled the ruins.
The man crept out to find her body and honour it
under the sickle-shaped moon.

Perhaps, one day the moon will cry
silver tears for all she sees
and move the Gods to stir up peace.

Summer Solstice

On the longest day when the sun stands still,
I have a conversation with Mannanán Mac Lir,
God of the oceans and of this inlet
where my house is poised.
I saw his chariot coming
drawn by Aonbarr,
a horse who gallops over Mannin Bay
as if the water was firm ground at the Curragh,
kicking up white waves as he goes.
Time has a different meaning
for Mannanán. He tells me
that the length of day is in your mind.
Joy mutes the ticking of a clock.
Grief slows it, almost unbearably.
It decants a day
leaving the sediment of sorrow.

The Gift

Sleek tip-to-tail
undulating otters,
two pups gambol in the water,
before they glide along
a jutting ridge of rock,
stopping to explore,
until ushered by mother
back into the incoming tide.
Long rudder tails,
opal-streaked evening light,
a mirroring sea
for one chiming moment
before its reverberations fade.
I understand what Adam lost
when he had to leave the Garden.

The Seals

They come to moult,
to copulate in a thrash of
swashbuckling water swords.
Here they birth their white-furred pups
where we share an inlet.
Mornings I will glance to see
if my spine of tidal rock
patched here and there with oarweed,
or mayweed maybe,
holds glistening mounds
humped up into a comfortable groove.
Their whiskered heads lift if I clump
to hang out washing, pegging shirts, socks
and one small scudding cloud.
When I bathe in seaweed off the rocks,
a seal treads water,
his mournful saucer eyes
watching this cumbrous creature splashing
in the element he speeds through
hardly rippling the surface.
Yet if I shed seven tears into high tide,
this selkie will shed his skin for me.

Vignette from Carcassonne

French grey on shutters, on walls,
on a t-shirt against sallow French skin.
I watch their greetings,
always respect from one to another,
the handshake, *ça va?*
Sometimes the double kiss.
The symphony of food,
art on a plate which may be fired glass
or art deco,
served and presented to honour the chef.

The man calling for *Pipette, Pipette,*
breath heaving, beret askew,
anxious, frantic,
while we watch wondering if it's dog, or child,
deciding it's *le chien.*
Then *le chat,* comes bounding guiltily
around a corner.
Ahead of us, also expecting *le chien,*
laughing too, are a French couple,
small and matched like a pair of porcelain figurines.

Pastille in F Sharp Minor

for Rod McGahon (1945-2015) who dared me write a poem about a sweet

I am not a poet,
I said,
I just write poetry.
He doffed his cap all the same.
Maybe he feared I'd write a satire
instead of a praise poem. He offered me a sweet,
a paler shade of purple.
I wondered if these were his favourites
and did he keep them to the packet's end.
His palate must be fine.
He spoke of crayfish
in black and amber bowls
and flinty dry wine.
I remembered the cave in the Loire valley
that I stumbled on.
The woman there had laryngitis
from the cold and damp
where she bottled and sold
the driest white in France –
madly sought after.
I only bought one bottle
of her champagne methode,
a rarefied ice tinkle in the mouth.
I didn't listen to Heraclitus
who said, *you can't step twice*
into the same stream.

Now the pianist, Antti Siirala,
makes his bow.
He sits and plays, *Time Shining*.
Single notes like sweets,
purple
pink
amber
silver
white
white
white.

The ABC of Connemara

Here also the woods are no more.
Traces of trees in bogs remain,
sessile oaks with grey furrowed bark,
dense hazel scrub rhymed by the hermit.

Unused is the secretive alphabet of the Druids
based on their sacred trees –
their first consonants B L N,
Beth-Luis-Nion, birch-rowan-ash.

Seasons are no longer marked with vowels.
There were dual vowels for Winter Solstice,
the birth tree, the death tree,
A and I, fir and yew.

Now I search for consonants and vowels
in the glacier-scoured landscape,
overwritten with scattered stunted trees,
which is my palimpsest.

This is November and I could choose from the stag I saw
engraved on the skyline at Crocnaraw,
who stood *en garde* bracketed with high-crowned antlers,
a medieval repository of trust;

or the burnt sienna of bracken's dying embers
vied with by *An Fheamainn Gheimhridh,* the Winter Weed,
glistening ruby red like a slashed pomegranate,
edged with the ruched russet of other tidal seaweeds.

Today there was the flight of plovers,
white-ringed, landing, refluttering,
resettling on a span of rock in a fuss of tutus
before taking off in formation down Mannin Bay,

skimming the mirroring water,
then wheeling in a silver flash
as the low sun caught their breast-feathers
in its applauding rays.

Mapping Millennia

Tap Tap Tap,
the delicate sound of fairy hammers
a dulled ping in the air of a blue day.
But it's student geologists
on Errislannan peninsula,
who tread on ancient rocks.
Perhaps they seek traces of the Iapetus Ocean
from Cambrian to Silurian periods
when it opened and closed,
some five hundred million years ago.
They read this landscape of Connemara,
record it with a wealth of words –
gneiss, gabbro, metasediment, strike-slip,
slickenside, tectonics, metamorphosis.
We live here in the framed layers of time.

The crow said 'Get Up'

– Jane Hirshfield

The crow says *Get Up,*
his caw raucous
before he scavenges
what's left behind, others' disasters.
My beak isn't reddened yet
but I'll scavenge amongst the poet masters.

The crow says *Get Up. Get Up.*
Stiff, I am as cumbersome
as a heron taking off.
Yet before others fingerprint
it on their early foray,
I may still get to touch and voice
this white-opal day.